I Know That!

Sound

Claire Llewellyn

Photography by Ray Moller

W
FRANKLIN WATTS
LONDON • SYDNEY

First published 2003 by Franklin Watts
96 Leonard Street, London EC2A 4XD

Franklin Watts Australia
45-51 Huntley Street
Alexandria, NSW 2015

Series advisor: Gill Matthews, non-fiction literacy consultant and Inset trainer
Editor: Rachel Cooke
Series design: Peter Scoulding
Designer: James Marks
Photography: Ray Moller unless otherwise credited

Acknowledgements: Stuart Baines/Ecoscene: 5b.
John Birdsall Photography: 5t. Derek Cattani/Eye Ubiquitous: 6l.
Bennett Dean/Eye Ubiquitous: 7tc. J.P. Ferrero/Ardea: 19t.
John Mielcarek/911 Pictures: 19b. Paula Solloway/Format/Photofusion: 21t.
Thanks to our models: Chloe Chetty, Nicole Davies, Georgia Farrell, Alex Green,
Madison Hanley, Aaron Hibbert, Chetan Johal, Henry Moller, Kane Yoon.

A CIP catalogue record for this book is available from the British Library

ISBN: 0 7496 5166 0

Printed in Malaysia

Contents

A world of sound

We live in a world
of sound.
We hear sounds all
around us.

▶ *We hear*
sounds at
home...

Shut your eyes and listen hard. What sounds can you hear all around you?

▲ *at school…*

◀ *in the street.*

Loud and soft

There are many different kinds of sound. Some sounds are loud. Others are soft.

◀*Crying*

Purring

Drilling

Very loud
sounds can hurt
our ears. The
man using the
drill is wearing
earmuffs
to protect
his ears.

Whispering

7

Making sounds

We make sounds every time we speak. We use our body to make other sounds, too!

▼ *"Hello!"*   ▼ *Pop!*   ▼ *Click!*

Try making these sounds with your body. What other sounds can you make?

◄ *Stamp!*

◄ *Clap!*

Making music

Musical instruments make all sorts of sounds. We play them in different ways.

◄ *We beat a drum...*

► *shake maracas...*

pluck a guitar...

How would you make these instruments sound soft? How would you make them sound loud?

blow into a recorder.

Hearing sounds

We hear with our ears. The shape of our ears helps us to hear well.

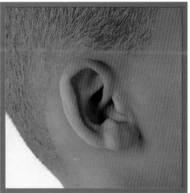

▶ *If we cup a hand around our ear, we can hear better.*

If we cover our ears, we can't hear as well.

Look at the ears of cats, rabbits and other animals. Which do you think is the best shape for hearing?

Where's that sound?

Our ears tell us where a
sound is coming from.
We do not need to
use our eyes.

Ring!
Ring!

▶ *We can hear the
phone in the bag…*

Knock! Knock!

▲ our friend at the window...

Miaow!

▶ the cat behind the chair.

Ask some friends to stand in a ring around you. Now close your eyes. Ask each person to make a short, soft sound. Can you point to where the sound is coming from?

15

Near or far?

Some sounds carry a long way.

▼ *A whistle sounds loud when we are near it…*

Ask a friend to stand next to you and make a sound. Now ask your friend to walk away slowly, and make the same sound after each step. How many steps does your friend take before you can't hear the sound any more?

◀ *and softer when we are far away.*

Warning sounds

Sounds can warn us of danger. They can help to keep us safe.

▶ *Ring! Ring! Make way!*

▲ *Grrrr! Don't touch!*

What sound
does a fire alarm
make? Why is it
good for warning
people?

◀*Nee-naa!
Clear the road!*

Sharing ideas

Sounds help us to
share ideas.
We share ideas when
we talk and listen.

▶ *We can
share a story.*

You don't need sound to share ideas. You can sign with your hands.

◀We can share a joke.

21

I know that...

1 There are many different sounds in the world around us.

2 Sounds can be loud or soft.

3 Sounds are made in many different ways.

▼"Hello!" ▼ Pop! ▼ Click!

4 We hear sounds with our ears.

5 Our ears tell us where a sound is coming from.

Ring! Ring!

6 A sound seems louder if you are close to it.

7 A sound seems softer from a long way away.

8 Sounds help to warn us of danger.

9 Sounds help us to share ideas.

Index

About this book

I Know That! is designed to introduce children to the process of gathering information and using reference books, one of the key skills needed to begin more formal learning at school. For this reason, each book's structure reflects the information books children will use later in their learning career – with key information in the main text and additional facts and ideas in the captions. The panels give an opportunity for further activities, ideas or discussions. The contents page and index are helpful reference guides.

The language is carefully chosen to be accessible to children just beginning to read. Illustrations support the text but also give information in their own right; active consideration and discussion of images is another key referencing skill. The main aim of the series is to build confidence – showing children how much they already know and giving them the ability to gather new information for themselves. With this in mind, the *I know that...* section at the end of the book is a simple way for children to revisit what they already know as well as what they have learnt from reading the book.